White Lies and a Kiss Goodbye

Diya Nijhawan

BookLeaf Publishing

India | USA | UK

Presentation by *BookLeaf Publishing*

Web: www.bookleafpub.com

E-mail: info@bookleafpub.com

ISBN: 978-93-5744-330-2

First edition 2021

DEDICATION

*20% of this book's royalties will be donated to
One Love Foundation.*

Distractions

Streetlights shine differently through window
blinds,
and seem to favor reflecting the red of stop
signs.

Our living room carpet is never completely
clean,
just start running your fingers in between.

Is it a bother how I fidget through this
interaction?
Perhaps not everything can be bent to your
satisfaction.

Why am I like this?

2

I crocheted this blanket a year ago,
and have watched it stand the test of time.

But tonight I fear that the yarn will unravel
under my big toe,
lost to the scene of the crime.

Unlearning

3

Those thoughts of yours became mine,
once our stars were forced to align.

That mess of yours was claimed as my own,
once it was one I could condone.

But I can't carry what you never showed me,
even if my mind tends to disagree.

The Promises I Keep

4

When my mother begged me to not go back to
you,
I told her not to worry because the person I
marry would be hers to review.

So I told myself not to be mad when that
promise was thrown in my face,
just allowed it to be another excuse for you to
treat me like a disgrace.

Maybe I was sorry then for being such a
challenge,
but I hope whoever loves me finds it easier to
manage.

Disparities

It took three months for you to consider commenting on the desirability of my body, and only three seconds for me to accept the apologies of your folly.

Hidden Words

In my ears, you whispered how life was altered
when we met,
while the world knew me as taking what you
could get.

Behind closed doors, I was read poetry in a
grand show of display,
but at dinner you didn't even tell your friends
that it was my birthday.

Now, these outsiders are noticing your
contradictions instead,
because the words said to me were never meant
to be spread.

The Moment I Left

Sometimes, I wonder if when you saw me again,
you remembered the embraces I was promised
back then.

But I prefer the version where it came as quite a
shock,
for you to realize this path was one I'd continue
to walk.

Decorations

The walls had been stripped bare,
rid of a comfort I couldn't repair.

Now, I'm in the room of my new apartment,
hanging the watercolors of a talented street
artist.

How I Survived

I didn't choose to have the ground crumble out
from underneath,
or free fall to the spaces that lay beneath.

I shut my eyes and braced for landing,
summoning a determination that was
nonwithstanding.

Was it love?

It's okay if some days it feels better to have
never been loved,
than admit how easily it can be misjudged.

After all, affections are already hard to accept,
once they've been laid with an intention of
disrespect.

Finding a Bare Minimum

I've learned to stop asking for what should be
expected,
once I remembered how to be respected.

Moments

Change is inevitable as a story will continue,
even if we don't like what it will hint to.

Refusing to move forward is not going to
preserve the good,
only allow those precious moments to be further
misunderstood.

Because nobody can give a lifetime on a single
night,
especially when operating on their pure delight.

Closure

13

I spent last night walking those familiar streets
alone,
remembering emotions that I've long outgrown.

My path then crossed with yours for the final
time,
and found no traces of our forgotten rhyme.

A Reminder

14

How special it is to create space for another
person to flourish,
allowing them to borrow parts of our courage.

Don't Gaslight Me

The truths that I know are not meant to be
influenced by others,
much less any potential lovers.

Therefore, I will never ask for your permission
to speak,
and will interrupt you if I want to critique.

I Can Walk Away

Love is never the necessity that I used to think it
was,
when I entertained those with me just because.

We no longer have to be perfect together,
if I can build a beautiful life for myself better.

Show Your Interest

I've learned to threaten the fear of rejection,
by daring them to walk in my direction.

Faults

18

Please continue to disappoint me,
your best isn't always a guarantee.

I'd rather have an honest conversation,
than one made by my imagination.

That's Not Cute

Happily ever after can't be designed only in your
eyes,
packed as my special surprise.

Lens of a Lover

Nobody will have to convince them of how
attractive you are,
as their ideal will never seem quite too far.

Just take care to not let their opinion influence
your own,
others are not worth discarding the only loves
you've ever known.

Title Advice

Believe it when they decide to leave you
neglected,
those white lies are meant to be dissected.

We'll send them a kiss goodbye in return,
and keep what is no longer their concern.

9 789357 443302

This collection was made to artfully deconstruct the difficulties of leaving. Please remember to practice self-care before, during, and after reading.

ABOUT THE AUTHOR

Diya is a US based poet currently studying at university. You can find her writing for new poetry prompts with the handle @musesofapoet on Instagram.

Presentation by *BookLeaf Publishing*

Web: www.bookleafpub.com

E-mail: info@bookleafpub.com

ISBN: 9789357211277

First edition 2022

DEDICATION

I dedicate this book for all the hopeless
romantics and old souls of the universe .

Courage and Time

In some lives they are together, in others they are lost in battle or become mere acquaintances destined to work together. I guess fate finds some balance between the princess and the noble knight to always meet .

Me

I love my eyes, my skin and my hair sometimes
I make changes that the world does not like and
sometimes it gives me very clear signs of that
but the sun and moon always remind me that I
do not harm the world

My Blue

3

His eyes turn days into nights
His hair is the softest I've ever touched
His face perfectly represented stars and planets
aligned
His lips could trapped sunsets with one single
kiss

Pink Skies

4

She will give you pink skies
She will give you kisses that taste like dark
chocolate
She will give you her heart with pink skies
ahead

Darkness

After all the darkness the princess was able to
see the moon again

Queen Of The Land

6

She served her people
She fed them
She listened to them
She loved them till the very end

Ramusr

My angel who once had a broken heart is flying
again
All my words went to him for so long
They would often asked who I would dress so
beautiful for
It was always for him
The ending was clear from the beginning he
wasn't for me
I loved him and I hope those kind words will
follow him always

Someday

8

I hope someday I can sit in their bedroom and
tell them I have met the one ..my prince

Nekuzo-Demon

She would become a demon out of nowhere
Her outstanding beauty would die in her demon
form
She had no remorse ,all signs of kindness would
disappear
She was demon that would destroy the whole
world now

Nekuzo-Human

Her beauty outshone the land
She was kind and loving
Her life was meant to be full of pain but her
story did contain a part where she lived and she
loved

Giselle

11

She was a lady that couldn't have her prince but she danced a whole night to save him from darkness

Starry Night

12

The stars and the moon cannot protect her when her heart gets broken but they can guide to her to healing

Brown Eyes …GB

You have those brown eyes that I will never
forget
You have that voice that will ring in my head
forever
If it's my curse to have you in my mind forever
then I shall die with it

The Sea

14

The sea is so blue these days
I wonder if the sea is picking up my feelings and
reflecting it to me

My Blue

15

My blue someday I will come to you with much
to say and with an ending to give me peace

My blue someday I will come to you with much
to say and with an ending to give me peace

White Rose

16

The white rose began losing it's petals and
slowly disappearing into the lake of memories

Ilia

17

She was sweet and kind
She would play in the gardens for fairies to see
She would heal him by giving him memories

Cloud 19

18

Clouds surrounded her hair and she was able to
rest
She started healing